FLIPPING THE
SWITCH

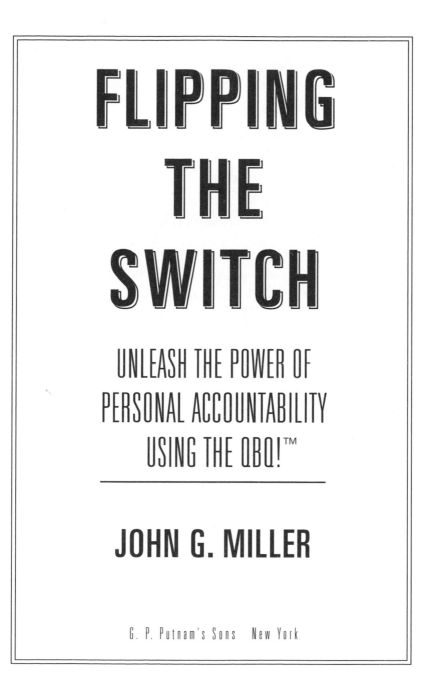

FLIPPING THE SWITCH

UNLEASH THE POWER OF PERSONAL ACCOUNTABILITY USING THE QBQ!™

JOHN G. MILLER

G. P. Putnam's Sons   New York

G. P. PUTNAM'S SONS
Publishers Since 1838
Published by the Penguin Group
Penguin Group (USA) Inc., 375 Hudson Street, New York, New York 10014, USA • Penguin
Group (Canada), 90 Eglinton Avenue East, Suite 700, Toronto, Ontario M4P 2Y3, Canada (a
division of Pearson Penguin Canada Inc.) • Penguin Books Ltd, 80 Strand, London WC2R
0RL, England • Penguin Ireland, 25 St Stephen's Green, Dublin 2, Ireland (a division of
Penguin Books Ltd) • Penguin Group (Australia), 250 Camberwell Road, Camberwell,
Victoria 3124, Australia (a division of Pearson Australia Group Pty Ltd) • Penguin Books
India Pvt Ltd, 11 Community Centre, Panchsheel Park, New Delhi–110 017, India • Penguin
Group (NZ), Cnr Airborne and Rosedale Roads, Albany, Auckland 1310,
New Zealand (a division of Pearson New Zealand Ltd) • Penguin
Books (South Africa) (Pty) Ltd, 24 Sturdee Avenue, Rosebank,
Johannesburg 2196, South Africa

Penguin Books Ltd, Registered Offices: 80 Strand, London WC2R 0RL, England

Library of Congress Cataloging-in-Publication Data

Miller, John G., date.
Flipping the switch—unleash the power of personal accountability
using the QBQ! / John G. Miller.
p.   cm.
A sequel to QBQ : the question behind the question (2001).
ISBN 0-399-15295-4
1. Choice (Psychology).   2. Decision making.   3. Problem solving.
4. Responsibility.   I. Title.
BF611.M55   2005   2004060248
153.8'3—dc22

Printed in the United States of America
5   7   9   10   8   6   4

This book is printed on acid-free paper. ∞

Acknowledgments

As we at QBQ, Inc., continue in our work to eliminate blame, complaining, and procrastination, we know we can never do it alone. We need you—our readers. I am continually amazed at the number of you who believe in personal accountability and know the world is a better place when each of us practices it. So heartfelt thanks go first to you for believing in QBQ!™

In addition, I want to extend my sincerest gratitude to those in my life who have made the difference for me:

David Levin, my writing partner, loyal buddy, and coach, who seems absolutely bent on finding ways to help me help others. I'd be nowhere without him.

Barry Neville, my literary agent. He knew, before all others, that the publishing world would be hungry to put the message of personal accountability into print. And he was right. In fact, he's right most of the time.

John Duff, a kind and gentle man at G. P. Putnam's Sons. His belief and friendship caused this "free spirit" and entrepreneurial author to become part of a larger team. Thanks to him, we can now reach the world.

· Acknowledgments ·

Husband-and-wife public relations team Jane Rohman and John Bianco. There is no way I can begin to measure their value. All they do is work hard, think creatively, and care. Not a bad combination for success.

Molly Hamaker, our writing expert. Her coaching and guidance—and editing—as we created this book drove us toward excellence.

Jim Strutton, who brought a high-energy twenty-seven-year-old with no sales or teaching experience into the training-and-development business. It was Jim who first took a chance on me.

My dad, Coach Miller to some and Pastor Jimmy to others. He seems to make it into every book we write. Though we lost him in 2002 at eighty, his impact remains—forever.

The children: Kristin, Tara, Michael, Molly, Charlene, Jazzy, and Tasha. A dad could not be more proud of his children than I am of the Sensational Seven. Thanks, guys, for making sure Dad's books are "face out" at every store you visit—and for being you.

And, most important, my wife since 1980—Karen. I asked her to go to the movies when disco was all the rage and we were only teens. It still is the best question I have ever asked. Thanks for saying "Yes!"

Karen, you will forever be my best friend.

Contents

—QBQ!—

· Contents ·

ADVANTAGE PRINCIPLE THREE · Creativity

ADVANTAGE PRINCIPLE FOUR · Service

· CONTENTS ·

ADVANTAGE PRINCIPLE FIVE • Trust

LIVING THE ADVANTAGE PRINCIPLES

CHAPTER ONE

The QBQ! Advantage Principles

=| QBQ! |=

I've seen firsthand the difference personal accountability can make. I recently had my first year-end evaluation from my new boss. In our organization—a large financial and insurance firm—the highest rating anyone can achieve on their performance review is an "Exceeds." My boss began the meeting by saying he had not awarded an "Exceeds" to anyone in fifteen years! "But your performance has been stellar and I'm giving you an 'Exceeds' rating for the year. I wish I had a dozen people just like you!"

In addition, his written comments said, "Consistently stays focused on the problem and how to make things better. Rarely criticizes others' performance, but instead works hard to improve communication within the department, understanding of the situation, and personal skills."

I honestly didn't know what to say, but that's when I realized how much QBQ! had helped me. I had read it just as I started in my new position, and it struck a chord with me. I took its lessons to heart and began to focus each day on how I could add value to a situation by asking better questions of myself. When I've been frustrated, the QBQ has helped me redirect my emotions toward contributing rather than complaining. I gained energy from identifying the things on which I could have an impact and then taking action on them. And now, one year later, my boss is commending me on the very areas in which I have been making an effort. What a tremendous feeling!

This story comes from Bill, a middle manager at a leading insurance firm and a reader of *QBQ! The Question Behind the Question.* And it illustrates perfectly what happens when someone "flips the switch." Flipping the switch means asking a QBQ (we'll cover the QBQ method in greater detail in chapter 2) and, simply put, those who use the QBQ and practice personal accountability have a better chance of succeeding than those who don't. I've come to think of it as the "QBQ Advantage." And though this particular story is about gaining an advantage at work, the QBQ and personal accountability bring similar advantages to every area of our lives.

In this book, we will explore the QBQ! Advantage Principles—five fundamental concepts or values that guide our behavior. The QBQ! Advantage Principles are:

Learning
Ownership
Creativity
Service
Trust

These principles aren't new, of course. Nor is the idea that living by them improves lives. What is new, and what we'll be exploring in this book, is how personal accountability and the QBQ relate to each of them. We'll show that using the QBQ and practicing personal accountability may be the most effective strategy for bringing the Advantage Principles to life.

But how is asking a QBQ like flipping a switch? Consider what happens when you turn on a light switch. It's so routine, you probably don't even think about it. When you flip the switch, you unblock—or unleash—a flow of electrons. This flow of energy, called a current, reaches the lightbulb in an instant, bringing it to life. Although the current lights the bulb, flipping the switch is the essential first step.

Similarly, asking a QBQ is the essential first step to bringing the Advantage Principles to life. Personal accountability is what powers the principles, but the QBQ is the switch that starts us thinking and acting accountably in the first place. Conversely, the bulb quickly darkens when we turn off the switch. The moment we stop being accountable—by blaming, complaining, thinking like a victim, or procrastinating—we *also* stop learning, taking ownership, acting creatively, or being of service. And the trust we've built with others will quickly evaporate.

So it's these five principles—Learning, Ownership, Creativity, Service, and Trust—that give us a tremendous advantage in our lives, but not without practicing personal accountability. And the QBQ helps us do just that.

But simply reading about personal accountability will not bring the Advantage Principles to life. Personal accountability is all about action—making better choices day in and day out. Throughout this book we'll hear stories of individuals like Bill who embody the Advantage Principles and see the difference personal accountability makes in their lives. But we won't see much difference in *our* lives until we take similar actions of our own. So let's start right now. As you read on, continually ask yourself, "How can I—how *will* I—apply these ideas at work and at home?" That's the first step toward unleashing the power of personal accountability and gaining the QBQ! Advantage. All it takes is the simple flip of a switch.

CHAPTER TWO

QBQ! The Question Behind the Question

═╢QBQ!╟═

Before getting into the first Advantage Principle, let's take a brief look at the QBQ, both as an introduction for those who haven't read *QBQ! The Question Behind the Question* and as a refresher for those who have. After all, repetition is the motor of learning!

QBQ stands for "the Question *Behind* the Question," and here's what it's all about: When faced with a problem or frustration, our minds first tend to fill with questions like "Why is this happening to me?" and "When will others do things right?" These questions are natural and understandable, but by focusing on everything and everyone except the person asking them, they demonstrate a lack of personal accountability. It's only when we stop and look *behind* those first questions that we find better ones—QBQs—such as "What can I do?" and "How can I contribute?" Asking these questions turns the focus back to ourselves and to what *we* can do to make a difference. It's nearly impossible to overstate the positive impact this simple change in focus can have on our lives!

To better understand the meaning and power of the QBQ, let's start by defining it. Then we will briefly explore key words contained within the definition.

*The QBQ is a **tool** that helps **leaders at all levels** practice **personal accountability** by **asking better questions** and making better **choices** in the moment.*

A TOOL

A tool is something we can use to help us—in the moment—perform at higher levels. Organizations have wasted billions of dollars on so-called tools that are really only motivational sessions, platitudes, and great-sounding fads. But when we get pumped up in our meetings, rallies, and seminars, and then have to go out to do our jobs—something happens: We hit the "wall of reality." We think, *What I heard in training sounded good, but it's not working for me in the real world.* In other words, it's not practical. And if it's not practical, it's not much of a tool.

The QBQ is different. It's practical *and* it works. What makes it work are three easy-to-apply guidelines that show us how to construct effective questions:

1. QBQs begin with the words "What" or "How," not "Why," "When," or "Who."
   - "Why" questions lead to complaining and victim thinking, as in, "Why is this happening to me?"
   - "When" questions lead to procrastination, as in, "When are they going to get back to me?"
   - "Who" questions lead to blame, as in, "Who dropped the ball?"
2. QBQs contain the word "I," not "they," "them," "you," or even "we," because I can change only *me.*
3. QBQs always focus on action.

One important point to keep in mind is that it is possible to apply the QBQ guidelines and still create a lousy question. For example, "How can I avoid responsibility in this matter?" or "What action can I take right now to hold the team back?" adhere to the rules, but they are certainly not constructive questions!

LEADERS AT ALL LEVELS

Leadership has nothing to do with our title, position, tenure, or "span of control" and everything to do with the way we think. By bringing responsibility, ownership, and action to life, the QBQ helps each of us think—and act—like a leader.

PERSONAL ACCOUNTABILITY

Personal accountability is about eliminating blame, complaining, and procrastination. When we point fingers looking for "whodunit," when we lament about our situation and what people are doing to us, and when we delay our own contribution while waiting for others to act, we are not putting personal accountability into action.

Everyone seems to agree on the need for personal accountability, but no one knows what to do about it.

The QBQ solves that problem by enabling us to transform our desire for accountability into real, lasting change.

ASKING BETTER QUESTIONS

The underlying concept of the QBQ is this:

The answers are in the questions.

When we ask better questions, we get better answers. The QBQ guidelines show us how to build better questions and which questions to avoid. Also, it's important to remember that these are questions we ask of *ourselves*, not of others. The QBQ is primarily a self-management tool, designed to help us reframe our *own* thinking.

CHOICES

We have countless opportunities each day to make choices. And what is it that we are always choosing? Our next thought. A compelling opportunity for change exists in these individual moments. Taking charge of our thoughts can literally transform our lives. By helping us make better choices, the QBQ enables us to do just that.

IQ/QBQ COMPARISONS

Incorrect Questions (IQs) are the "why," "when," and "who" questions that lead to victim thinking, procrastination, and blame. Contrasting QBQs with IQs is an excellent way to learn how to put the QBQ into action. Let's take a look at the following IQ/QBQ comparisons:

> *The sale falls through.*
> IQ: "When will I ever get a break?"
> QBQ: "How can I better understand my customer?"

> *You're passed over for a promotion.*
> IQ: "Why did this happen to me?"
> QBQ: "What can I do in my current job to excel?"

> *Our child struggles in school.*
> IQ: "Why can't the schools be more effective?"
> QBQ: "How can I help him succeed?"

The people you manage fail to do their jobs.
IQ: "Why aren't they motivated?"
QBQ: "How can I improve my coaching skills?"

A mistake is made.
IQ: "Who blew it?"
QBQ: "What can I do to help solve the problem?"

For a complete exploration of the QBQ, I encourage you to read *QBQ! The Question Behind the Question.*

Before we go on to the first Advantage Principle, take a moment to review the IQ/QBQ comparisons one by one. Think about how you might make better choices and ask better questions. Consider the impact of eliminating blame, complaining, victim thinking, and procrastination. Imagine the difference the QBQ will make in *your* life, both at work and at home.

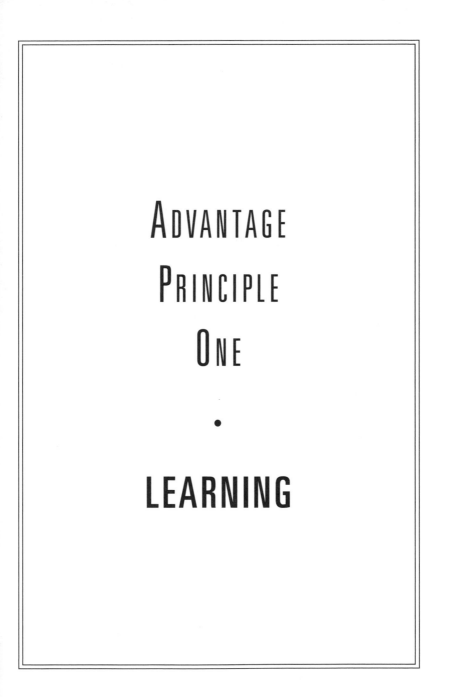

ADVANTAGE

PRINCIPLE

ONE

·

LEARNING

CHAPTER THREE

A Picture of Learning

=[QBQ!]=

Following a presentation I made to a travel company some years ago, a young man named David came up to me and asked, "Mr. Miller, have you written any books?"

At that time, I hadn't, so I said, "No, not yet, but I will soon. Why do you ask?"

"I just thought if I had some way to study your material further," David replied, "I could apply it even better!"

Although this exchange happened years ago, I still remember how impressed I was with David's commitment to learning. I thanked him and said I'd send him a copy of my first book when it came out.

Afterward, we all moved to another room for the company's annual awards banquet. When dinner was over, the CEO got up and began lauding people for their achievements. One by one they came forward to receive their recognition, a parade of smiling achievers smothered in the applause of their peers.

Finally, it came time to announce the Top Agent of the Year award, honoring the individual who not only produced outstanding revenue but also demonstrated exceptional leadership. The CEO paused for effect. The tension was high. When she finally announced the name, we all stood and cheered for— you guessed it—David!

I have no proof, but I firmly believe there is a direct correlation between David's commitment to Learning and the fact that he was the firm's top achiever. His success wasn't based on luck, height, heritage, family background, or good looks. Rather, it was based on his desire to study more and a genuine desire to continually learn, change, and grow.

A Learning mentality can be a powerful advantage in each of our lives. It enhances our ability to adapt to change, reach the goals we've set, and become the people we wish to be. It helps our work, teams, and organizations to be more innovative, productive, and fun. But perhaps what is most important is how it makes us feel. Learning brings forth energy, enthusiasm, and a zest for life that's lacking in those who—for whatever reason—have ceased to learn.

We are *not* Learning when we ask the IQs:

"When is someone going to train me?"
"Why do we have to go through all this change?"
"When are we going to hear something new?"
"Who's going to give us the vision?"
"Why can't others do their jobs right?"

We *are* Learning when we ask the QBQs:

"What can I do to develop new skills?"
"How can I adapt to the changing world?"
"What can I do to apply what I'm hearing?"
"How can I be more productive today?"
"What can I do to be my best?"

How can we become more like David? By asking QBQs that open our minds and help us embrace change. And that's when we start practicing the Advantage Principle of Learning!

CHAPTER FOUR

Garbage Thinking:
The Roadblocks to Learning

QBQ!

What would you say if I told you I have a friend who never takes out his garbage? Instead he keeps it stored in drawers, plastic containers, and boxes. From time to time he pulls it out, spreads it on the floor, and rolls in it—for hours. I imagine you'd say that purposely collecting, hoarding, and wallowing in garbage is a ridiculous—even insane—thing to do. And I'd agree. Yet we all do it—maybe not literally, like my fictional friend, but in *our minds*.

Since 1986, I've spent thousands of hours conducting training sessions for organizations and groups of all kinds. During that time, I've come to recognize that every one of us holds on to "garbage" thoughts, ideas, and viewpoints that close our minds and keep us off the path of personal growth. This garbage thinking manifests in many ways, but each tends to fit into one of five categories, or mindsets, which I call the Roadblocks to Learning. They are:

Exception Mentality
Expectations
Entitlement Thinking
Experience Trap
Exclusion

To bring the advantages of the Principle of Learning into our lives, we must first eliminate these roadblocks from our thinking. Let's look at how the QBQ can help us do that.

ROADBLOCK ONE: EXCEPTION MENTALITY

Flying to Kansas City from St. Louis one evening, about a one-hour flight, I used my frequent flier miles to upgrade to first class. As I took my seat, I smiled and said "Hello" to the gentleman next to me.

He smiled back. After I settled in, I noticed the cuff links, starched white shirt, full dark suit, deep maroon tie, and wing tips, and I immediately knew whom I was sitting next to: *an executive.*

We began chatting, and I learned he was a senior vice president with a Fortune 100 firm. I pulled out a *QBQ!* book and gave it to him. He thanked me but said he'd need to look at it later as he had a presentation to prepare for the next day. However, I was soon delighted to see that he started reading it anyway and continued until we landed. But I didn't say a word. I just kept my nose in my *USA Today.*

Just before we pulled into the gate, he leaned toward me, pointing at a sentence in the book. I looked and it was the QBQ "What can I do?" He then asked, "Why couldn't that say, 'What can *we* do?'"

"Well," I said, "I've learned over the years that I can't change the 'we' but I *can* change me."

He nodded seriously, reflected for a moment, and then said: "You know what? My *boss* needs to read this book!"

I still laugh thinking about it. What a great example of the Exception Mentality: "This content on personal accountability is really great, but it certainly doesn't apply to *me!*"

There's a lesson here we should all keep in mind:

We tend to teach to others what we need to hear ourselves.

Meaning: If we hear an idea and immediately think of *other* people who really need it, that's a good sign *we* may need the idea more than they do. This can be a challenging concept, but one I've certainly found to be true in my own life. Whenever I look at Child Number Four in our house (daughter Molly) and wonder, *Why is she so stubborn and inflexible?* my mind freezes and I'm transported back in time, thinking, *Hmm, didn't someone say those words to me thirty years ago, or thirty days ago, or even thirty minutes ago?* Yes, we tend to teach to others what we need to hear ourselves.

Don't let the Exception Mentality roadblock stand in your way. When you think, *I really know someone who needs to hear this,* stop and consider if you can apply it to yourself first by asking the QBQ "How can I use this in my life?"

ROADBLOCK TWO: EXPECTATIONS

It's difficult to expand a closed mind. I was talking with my neighbor over the back fence one day. He told me how he had recently endured a three-day training session offered by his company that was "boring, irrelevant, and a waste of time." His most revealing comment, though, was this: "I wasn't surprised. *I knew it wouldn't be any good.*"

We usually find what we are looking for. Negative expectations such as "This isn't going to be any good" can be self-fulfilling prophecies. They keep us from learning, growing, and enjoying life. Even if our last experience was "boring," it doesn't necessarily mean the next one will be, too.

Keep an open mind. Expect to learn. Ask a QBQ like "How can I gain the most from today?"

ROADBLOCK THREE: ENTITLEMENT THINKING

When our daughter Tara (Child Number Two) was twelve, she came to me early one morning with a tooth in her hand. My first thought was *When does this end?* My next thought was *Tara, is that a recycled tooth you're trying to sell me?* (As parents, we do have to be careful we don't pay for the same tooth twice, don't we?) But I knew what she wanted, so I said, "Come on, honey, you know what to do. Just put that tooth under your pillow tonight, and if you're lucky the tooth fairy might leave you a little something." The preteen looked at me as if I had missed a memo. Then she stuck out her hand a little farther and said, "Dad, don't waste my time—I gotta go. Give me a break and give me a buck!"

That's Entitlement Thinking, and while it was funny with Tara, there's too much of it in our organizations. You can hear it in the new hire who says, "I've been here three months—when am I going get my first *annual* increase?" and in the veteran who declares, "I've been here twenty-two years, so I deserve . . . !"

This may sound harsh, but honestly, if someone's worked and been paid for twenty-two years, wasn't that the agreement? Don't get me wrong—loyalty is a good thing—but I have a hard time understanding why we feel we deserve something more or different just because we've been around a long time.

Another area where Entitlement Thinking abounds is in our attitude toward training and development. When we ask people, "Who's responsible for your personal development?" they say, "I am." And yet so often we hear people ask, "When am I going to get more training?" Now, I believe it's a manager's job each day to ask the QBQ, "What can I do today to develop my people?" But no one owes us training. In the end, the responsibility for my lifelong change journey is mine alone. So watch out for thoughts like, "My manager *should* coach me more!" or "My organization *should* provide me more training!" They prevent us from taking action and become roadblocks to Learning.

"When is someone going to train me?" is the wrong question. The better questions are QBQs such as "What can I do to invest in myself?" and "How can I acquire new knowledge to meet the challenges ahead?"

ROADBLOCK FOUR: EXPERIENCE TRAP

For those who think they've "made it"—or arrived—
I have one word: *Titanic!* The sinking of that supposedly "unsinkable" ship in 1912 is the classic
picture of human arrogance and overconfidence
meeting the unknown. Each day we, too, meet the
unknown. And though our experience should be
our window to understanding and wisdom, too
often it is the basis for thinking we've completed the
voyage. The Experience Trap prevents personal
growth and change from occurring by allowing us to
think we know all there is to know. Consider these
examples:

- The manager who emulates the style of a former boss without considering what works best
  with today's workforce
- The tenured teacher who refuses to embrace
  new ways of helping students learn
- The salesperson trained in the "slap 'em on the
  back and take 'em to lunch" style of selling
  who won't adopt modern sales tactics

- The parents of a highly successful child who resist finding the right approach with their other children
- The executive who performed well in one industry, but fails to understand the differences and nuances of a new one
- The person who uses the Seven Sinful Words: "We've never done it that way before."

The way to drive Learning—and there's always more to learn—is to keep asking, "How can I enhance my effectiveness?" and "What can I do to acquire new skills?" These QBQs are a powerful defense against the Experience Trap—and keep us squarely on the path of personal growth and change.

ROADBLOCK FIVE: EXCLUSION

One day, soon after I started speaking on personal accountability and the QBQ, I came down from the platform after a talk to shake some hands and enjoy the moment. I was feeling particularly good because

I thought it was one of the best presentations I'd ever delivered, and the response from the audience seemed to confirm my impressions.

After the excitement had died down and the crowd had left, I noticed one person still in the ballroom whose face clearly told me she was underwhelmed. She was the one who had coordinated the meeting, and I certainly wanted her feedback. After a little coaxing, she gave me her critique: There was something about my style of delivery that interfered with the message. She simply did not like it. I smiled and thanked her for her candor. But let me tell you what I was really thinking. It's not pretty, but it's real: *What do you know? You're not a salesperson or a speaker. You've never done what I just did!*

I did not hear her because I *excluded* her. I eroded her credentials, marginalized her input, and dismissed her criticism because I believed she couldn't possibly understand what it's like to do what I do. Through my own arrogance and prejudice, I decided she didn't "belong to my group," and, thus, her opinion was unworthy.

As I flew home that evening, though, I considered her input and admitted to myself that her point was valid. She was right. She had shared an insight that, as it turned out, helped me a great deal when I decided to apply it later.

We use Exclusion every day against people who are different from ourselves, in all walks of life. Consider these scenarios:

- The salesperson rejects what the marketing person says because "He's never been in the field."
- The manufacturing people dismiss the sales team's perspective, thinking *You have no clue what we do or how hard it is to do it!*
- The executive doesn't listen to the administrative assistant because "Well, what could she possibly know?"
- The doctor doesn't hear the nurse because she's thinking *She didn't go to medical school for twelve years.*
- The parent ignores the child's opinion because "Parents always know best."

We're all students. We're all teachers. There are valuable lessons to be learned everywhere we turn. But we will miss the opportunity when we engage in Exclusion. Let's avoid this roadblock by asking, "How can I truly listen and consider applying what this person has to say?"

· CHAPTER FIVE ·

QBQ! Learning Equals Change

$$\boxed{\text{QBQ!}}$$

This story comes from Robin, an anesthesiologist for a maternity unit in Auckland, New Zealand. Robin consults with mothers, performs procedures, and is available for emergency deliveries. She also has a leadership role within her hospital.

One Monday morning around 3 A.M., I was called to the hospital to perform an epidural on a very distressed mother who was in the middle of a tough labor.

The midwife had tried and failed to insert an intra-venous line, so I had an additional procedure to perform before I could do the epidural. And I had some trouble with it, too.

Suddenly, just after I had secured the IV line, the mother said, "I want to push!" The midwife did a quick examination and confirmed she was about to deliver. "I'm sorry," she told me, slightly embarrassed. "We don't need the epidural after all." "That's wonderful!" I responded. The midwife stared at me. Her eyes seemed to say, "What's the catch?" She was probably thinking Who are you, and what have you done with the real Robin?

I used to get angry in these situations—being called all the way to the hospital, then turned away because someone had misjudged the labor. "Stupid midwives!" I'd want to shout. But now—since reading QBQ!—when these things happen I find joy by focusing on the positives. In this case, the labor was going better than expected, a medical intervention wasn't needed after all, and I could get back to bed that much sooner. Also, the midwife was doing her very best. Medicine is unpredictable, and these surprises happen all the time. And on this morning, my presence alone gave the mother the support she needed to be able to bear the pain just a little longer.

Later that day, the same midwife came to me and asked, "Can I talk to you, please? There's an issue that's been bothering me." We then discussed a problem that had persisted for some time, which involved differing perspectives between midwives and doctors. After we talked it through, she volunteered to do a whole pile of things that supported the strategies we as a leadership team had already planned to implement.

This may not sound like much, but she'd never approached me like that before. I was actually taken aback at first. What was this about? Why the sudden change? But then I realized—I had changed. I had used the QBQ to be more positive, and that's why she suddenly felt comfortable coming to me. Now we have her onboard with our new program. That's teamwork. And around here, teamwork is everything!

By choosing to be personally accountable, I have clearly gained something precious in my life. Thank you!

This story is an excellent illustration of the difference between simply gaining knowledge and true Learning. Do you remember pulling an "all-nighter" to cram for an 8 A.M. exam, taking it, and then knowing virtually nothing when it was over? Storage of facts and theories in our temporal memory might get us by in school, but it's not Learning. Real Learning happens when we turn *knowing* what to do into *doing* what we know. In other words, Learning equals change.

Robin could have discovered the QBQ and done

nothing with it. She might have succumbed to road-blocks like the Exception Mentality ("Good stuff, but it doesn't apply to me") or the Experience Trap ("I'm good at what I do and don't need this"). But, instead, by choosing to put her new knowledge into action, she became a QBQ! Learner. And by changing her behavior, she "gained something precious" in her life. Robin's story isn't a dramatic one that changed the world. But it changed *her* world, and that's what's important.

When you ask the QBQ and put knowledge into action, the Advantage Principle of Learning can change your world, too.

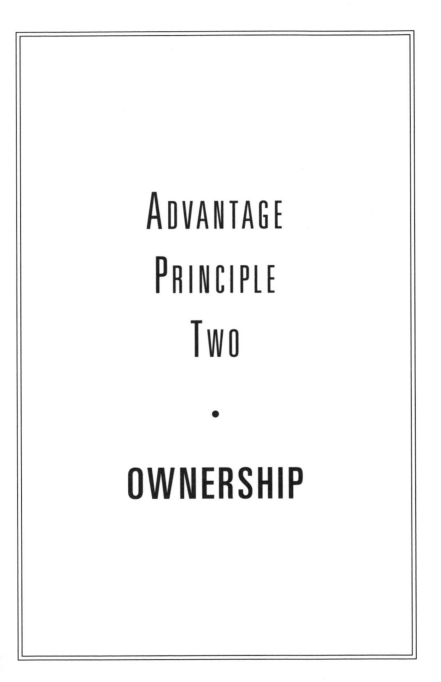

ADVANTAGE PRINCIPLE TWO

·

OWNERSHIP

CHAPTER SIX

Ownership:
Solve the Problem!

—QBQ!—

Sarah's Story

As a new employee at a fast-paced, high-stress mortgage company, Sarah hadn't turned in her "new hire" forms to the payroll department on time. So when her first payday rolled around—no check. That's a problem. When her boss, the branch manager, heard about it and put in a call to the home office, she was asked, "Who made the mistake on her paperwork?" Upon hearing that, the manager responded with this simple yet powerful statement: "I'm not sure, but if it gets Sarah her check, then *I* did!" What she was really saying was "Who cares *who* did it? *Let's solve the problem!*"

Diane's Story

Diane, a *QBQ!* reader, shares this story: "I landed late one evening, around eleven o'clock, at the Richmond, Virginia, airport. Just my luck, there were three shuttle buses lined up at the curb heading to parking lots in other directions, but none to my lot. After the first two departed, the third one pulled up and its door opened. The driver yelled, 'Hi, I'm Sherry. If you want to go to the A lot, don't read what the sign on my bus says, just hop right in!' As I did, I asked if some buses had stopped running. She said no, but a few drivers had missed their stops, so things were all messed up. Laughing, she continued, 'Some drivers just don't get it, but I figure since you're standing there looking tired, and I'm sitting here with no place to go, we should just go to A together!'"

Stan's Story

Stan Donnelly is the founder and CEO of Donnelly Custom Manufacturing Company of Alexandria, Minnesota, which molds plastic parts for all kinds of products. For one project, they created latches and clips for another manufacturer's new in-line skates. Unfortunately, someone at Donnelly attached the latches to the skates backward—a simple error that slipped by unnoticed.

When a small team from the skate manufacturer—including the company's president—took several pairs of skates to Europe to call on a potential distributor, they opened the boxes and were surprised to find that the latches did not work. Big problem. Word got back to the Donnelly organization, and the project team discussed what had happened. One person asked the IQ "Why didn't they look at the skates more closely before they left the country?"

"No," Stan answered forcefully, "that was *our* job!"

These three stories are all great examples of Ownership in action. Ownership does not require having an equity stake in the organization or holding an official position of leadership. It simply means facing problems head-on instead of blaming, complaining, procrastinating, or making excuses. Ownership is personal accountability in its purest form, and the QBQ helps bring it to life.

We do *not* take Ownership when we ask the IQs:

"When will they take care of this?"
"Who dropped the ball?"
"Why don't they improve things around here?"
"Who's going to clarify my job?"
"Why is there so much blame?"

We *do* take Ownership when we ask the QBQs:

"How can I solve the problem?"
"What can I do to contribute?"
"How can I help the organization succeed?"
"What can I do to expand my personal impact?"
"How can I rid blame from my life?"

We need Ownership because organizations have problems—things go wrong, mistakes are made—and problems need to be solved. Of course, we no longer call them *problems*. We now call them "opportunities," "issues," and "situations." On some days, we feel as if we're buried in *challenges*! But whatever we call them, they're still problems. And we gain a distinct advantage when we practice the Principle of Ownership—because only then do we find solutions.

CHAPTER SEVEN

The Blame Game:
The Opposite of Ownership

—QBQ!—

Fast food is blamed for obesity. Youth violence is blamed on computer games. Politicians blame one another for our country's problems. Hollywood is blamed for our culture of "moral decay."

Some days it seems the blame game is the only game in town. Everybody is pointing fingers at everybody else. But wait! Before we get too focused on all the blame "out there," consider these questions:

- When I was late to work, did I blame the morning traffic?
- When my child's grades fell, did I blame the teachers?
- When I lost my job, did I blame the president?

- When I returned a call late, did I say, "I've just been so busy"?
- When I was in a bad mood, did I blame my family and coworkers for my feelings?
- When the sale fell through, did I blame our product pricing or the customer?
- When I got a poor test grade, did I blame the professor's teaching style?
- When my customer didn't get the product on time, did I blame the shipping department?
- When my portfolio crashed, did I blame my broker?
- When my son got into trouble, did I blame the friends he hangs out with?
- When my drive put the ball into the rough, did I blame the wind?
- When my place of worship failed to thrive, did I blame its leadership?
- When I forgot to follow through on a promise, did I say, "Life is too hectic"?
- When our Little League team lost Saturday's game, did I blame the officials?
- When I didn't get a raise (or my benefits were reduced), did I blame management?

- When the project didn't get completed on time, did I blame the team?

Blame is a natural response. Everyone slips into it now and then, myself included. And though blame is an obvious waste of time, I've yet to come across an organization or segment of society that's immune from it.

BLAME SOLVES NO PROBLEMS

The following is one of those "forwards" that has been passed on by who-knows-how-many people before showing up in your e-mail box. This one is the voice mail greeting supposedly installed by a high school's staff in response to a lawsuit brought by parents over failing grades and low achievement test scores:

Hello! You have reached the automated answering service for your school. Please listen to all your options before making a selection:

To lie about why your child is absent, press 1.

To make excuses for why your child did not do his work, press 2.

To complain about how we do things, press 3.

To swear at staff members, press 4.

To ask why you didn't get information that was actually enclosed in our newsletter and sent home with the student, press 5.

If you want us to raise your child, press 6.

If you want to reach out and slap someone, press 7.

To request another teacher for the third time this year, press 8.

To gripe about bus transportation, press 9.

To complain about school lunches, press 0.

But if you realize that your child is accountable and responsible for his or her own behavior, class work, and homework—and that it's not the teacher's fault for your child's lack of effort and achievement—please hang up now and have a nice day!

Pretty funny. From what I can gather, it's an anonymous piece of fiction that spread like wildfire across the Internet. But it's still a sad commentary on education in our country. It's also a powerful illustration of the futility of blame: *Blaming others about our kids' education is never going to solve the problem.*

Blame never solves *any* problem, because we can't play the blame game and take Ownership at the same time. And without Ownership, nothing gets done, nothing is fixed, and nothing improves.

CHAPTER EIGHT

A Study in Blame: E-Mail Wars

—|QBQ!|—

There we are, hunkered down in our cubicle, corner office, or field site. It's trench warfare! In the glow of the computer screen, we loft an e-mail volley to the other side, hoping their return shot will miss the mark—exposing a fatal flaw in their argument—so we can eagerly copy all the troops and commanders on our reply. Success will be ours! Victory, so sweet!

This scenario, while admittedly over the top, illustrates a problem that is all too real and tremendously expensive—infighting, which is just another form of blame. There may not be lines for "feuding with coworkers" and "blaming other departments" on the balance sheet, but the cost to teamwork, morale, and productivity is there. So not only does blame fail to solve problems, it also significantly *adds* to them.

We can do better. Let's stop fighting with each other and start fighting our problems instead.

CHAPTER NINE

No Excuses

=QBQ!=

When I was a teenage driver, my parents drilled this idea into my head: Watch the other guy! What they meant was that everyone commits mental errors on the road—so not only should I be concerned with myself, but also I should watch out for the other drivers' mistakes. I imagine you heard a similar message. And like so much else my parents told me, it turned out to be pretty smart advice after all. Here's a little gem I still remember and have taught to my children, too:

> *Here lies the body of Jonathan J.,*
> *Who died maintaining the right-of-way.*
> *He was right, dead right, as he rode along,*
> *But just as dead as if he had been wrong!*

Safe driving is pure personal accountability and Ownership in action. It's our responsibility to be aware of our surroundings and circumstances at all times and to carefully operate the vehicle. For example, if I ram someone from behind, *I am always responsible.* It doesn't matter why the car ahead of me brakes—the accident is *always* my fault, because I should have been at a safe enough distance behind to have time to respond to anything that could happen. It's a "no excuses" moment.

Beyond driving, when someone falls off a stepladder while changing a lightbulb or loses a toe to a running lawn mower—it's the same truth: At work, at home, and behind the wheel, personal safety is always the responsibility of the individual. So the next time you trip over a child's toy on the living room floor or catch your foot on a kitchen chair, don't make excuses by asking the IQs "Why can't the kids pick up their stuff?" and "Who put that stupid chair there?" Practice Ownership instead. Ask QBQs such as "What can I do to own the situation?" and "How can I be more careful?"

CHAPTER TEN

The Ultimate Excuse: It's Not My Job

— QBQ! —

I checked into a Scottsdale, Arizona, conference resort late one night for a speaking engagement at 8 A.M. the next day in front of three hundred pharmaceutical sales professionals. After scoping out the ballroom, I realized I'd be speaking from a fairly high platform, which meant my shoes would be right at eye level to the audience. Knowing that pharmaceutical reps tend to be an especially well dressed group and would probably all be wearing brightly shined shoes, I asked a person at the front desk, "Any chance I can get my shoes polished here tonight?"

"Mr. Miller, here's what I can do: I'll run down to the drugstore and buy some polish because I don't believe we have any here. Or, the valet could take them over to the resort across the highway, where they have a shoeshine stand that's open until midnight. Or, I could take them home with me, polish them at my house, and bring them back around 7 A.M. when I start my next shift. Would any of these options be satisfactory for you, Mr. Miller?"

Can you imagine? How would you have responded? "Fantastic! Thanks!" And how would you feel about him and his establishment? Would you remember his name? Would you be telling all your friends about him and his resort? Yes, I'm sure you would, just as I'm telling you now.

Well, I'm sorry to let you down, but this never happened—at least not that way. Nor did I expect the front-desk clerk to offer any of these solutions. But I did ask if I could get my shoes polished, and the conversation went more like this:

Me: "Any chance I can get my shoes polished here tonight?"
Him: "Nope."
The end.

Is he a bad person? No, not at all. I wouldn't expect anyone to take my shoes home and polish them on their own time. I'm simply saying that taking Ownership of my problem *never even crossed his mind*. As far as I could tell, he just didn't care, which is about the worst message you could send in the service industry. Now, it's possible I got it wrong. Maybe he did care but was only thinking, *I don't shine shoes*. In other words, the Ultimate Excuse: "It's not my job."

A job description—an outline detailing our specific roles and responsibilities—is a marvelous tool. But it can also become an excuse for not owning the problem at hand. It can keep us from finding creative solutions and cause others to think we don't care. Nowhere in this employee's job description did it say, "Shoe shining," so that was the end of that.

Our jobs don't end at the last period of the last word in the last sentence of our job description. Don't say, "It's not my job!" Take Ownership of problems. Show others you care. Be creative. Gain that extra edge by going that extra mile. Ask the QBQ, "How can I help this person right now?"

CHAPTER ELEVEN

Owning Safety

━━ QBQ! ━━

Sometimes a problem or situation can be owned by the wrong people. Ron Pote, an expert on safety in the workplace, told me this story:

When I was the department manager of a large and inherently dangerous paper mill, I got a call at 5 A.M. on a Tuesday morning. Steve, one of my night-shift guys, was hurt. Within thirty minutes I met his terrified wife and three crying children at the hospital. He had a broken arm, fractured skull, and numerous lacerations. He was in really bad shape but would live.

What happened was this: Steve had removed a metal protective screen from a large piece of equipment so he could reach in to make an adjustment. That's when his shirtsleeve caught on a rotating shaft and pulled him in. Honestly, he could've been killed.

When I heard what he had done, my first thoughts were Why would Steve do such a thing? Why would he take a chance like that and risk his own safety? *I just couldn't understand why someone would violate the company's safety policy by removing protective guards. Steve was a model employee and should have known better. What was he thinking?*

And then it hit me: Steve and his family were now suffering because of the culture I—and others in management—had created. We had a safety program in place, but too much of it involved just slapping slogans on the wall and lecturing employees endlessly in meetings. Bluntly put, our program left Ownership for safety more to managers than the front-line people. It was clear that greater responsibility needed to be shifted to those who would ultimately bear the consequences of an unsafe action. As managers, we would never be able to prevent accidents like Steve's, because we could not be in all places at all times to make all the decisions. If our safety record was to further improve, individuals needed to watch out for themselves— and their teammates.

Thus began a renewed effort to get people to take Ownership of their own safety. We implemented specific one-on-one coaching sessions with all employees, emphasizing individual safety responsibilities. We confronted any employee who didn't grasp that message and re-coached them, and hammered home the message with memos, meetings, and casual conversations with people. We started to see a real improvement and, as managers, came to understand that safety only improves when we broaden our focus beyond rules, procedures, equipment, and systems to include each team member's personal accountability for choices made to work safely—or not.

It took about three years to change the safety culture of my department and the plant. But now managers and *employees understand that each of us must take Ownership for our personal on-the-job safety. Every moment. No excuses.*

CHAPTER TWELVE

Taking Ownership Too Far

— QBQ! —

Ownership is the first step to solving problems, which is essential to making a difference in our organizations and our lives. But any strength taken to an extreme becomes a weakness. Ownership is *not*:

- Doing the work of others
- Rescuing people who aren't performing
- Saying "Okay, it's my fault!" whenever something goes wrong
- Trying to fix everything alone

Take Ownership, but don't take it too far. Ask QBQs like "How can I contribute?" and "What can I do to help others reach their goals?" But remember: Not every problem is ours alone to solve.

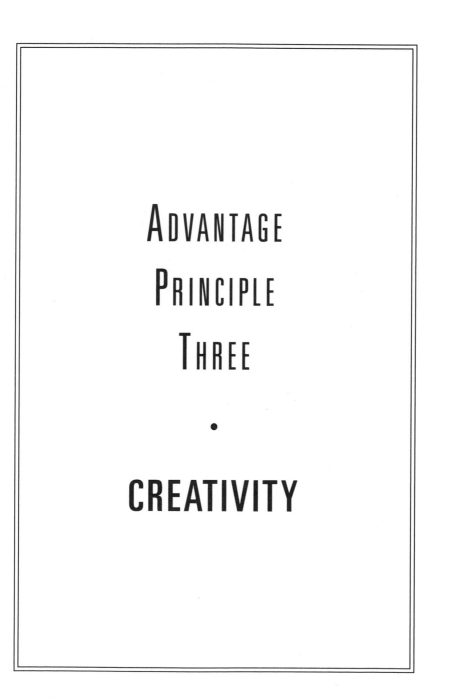

ADVANTAGE
PRINCIPLE
THREE

·

CREATIVITY

CHAPTER THIRTEEN

QBQ! Creativity: Succeeding with What We Have

— QBQ! —

When Kristin and Tara, our two oldest children, were about eleven and nine, they asked to be driven to the store to buy a really fun game they'd played at a friend's house. When we got there, they quickly discovered it cost about six dollars more than they had. They were stuck, but they didn't look to me for help.

The reason they didn't ask Dad to bail them out is this: My wife, Karen, and I use a financial system with our kids in which starting at age nine they begin handling their own money. We fund a monthly "budget" for them that provides money in five categories: savings, charity, gifts (for birthdays and holidays), miscellaneous, and clothing. Yes, clothing. The children—not Mom and Dad—for many years now have paid for their own jeans, shirts, dress clothes, winter coats, and shoes. It's gratifying to watch our now teenaged girls search for bargains instead of expensive, trendy clothing. There's also no reaching into Mom's purse for plastic money or arguments over what to buy. They have their own money and know if they spend it all before the month is over, they wait until next month for more. No exceptions. As they would put it, "When it's gone—*it's gone!*"

Leaving the store, the girls were disappointed. But shortly after we got home, I heard giggling from the other room. The girls would run into the kitchen for supplies and quickly disappear again. Whatever they were doing, they were clearly having a great time. And what do you think was going on? They were making their own version of the game! For the next couple of hours the whole family enjoyed playing the game they had created.

I can hardly imagine a better example of Creativity. I don't think it ever would have occurred to me to make the game at home, but they were undeterred by a lack of resources. They put their heads together and came up with a wonderful solution.

Normally when we think of Creativity, we think of artistic skills such as writing, drawing, or painting. But facing an obstacle and coming up with another way to reach the goal is Creativity at its finest.

We do *not* employ Creativity when we ask the IQs:

"Why don't we get more tools to do our job?"
"Who's going to get me the information I need?"
"When will we get better systems?"
"When will I find reliable, committed
    people?"
"Why don't I get a bigger budget?"

We *do* employ Creativity when we ask the QBQs:

"What can I do to succeed with the tools I have?"
"How can I obtain the information required?"
"What action can I take to move forward?"
"How can I develop the people I have?"
"What can I do to reach the goal?"

Creativity is a tremendous advantage in achieving our goals. The road to success is rarely smooth and obstacle-free. There are potholes to dodge, barriers to leap, and muddy roads to travel. But where others get stuck and give up, people who use Creativity stay focused on the goal and keep working until they discover the path to success, both at work and at home.

CHAPTER FOURTEEN

A Creative Shift in Thinking

$$\boxed{\text{QBQ!}}$$

Bob Bonkiewicz is an exceptional salesperson who worked with me in the training-and-development field. Bob had a unique approach. We used to kid him about traveling light. When he went on sales calls, he carried only two items: a legal tablet and a Crayola marking pen. (Not a crayon, but close.)

Once comfortably settled in the office of a vice president or a CEO, Bob would take his pen, draw a circle in the upper left corner of his yellow pad, write the word "Leadership" in it, and say, "We work in the area of leadership development." Then he'd draw another circle, write "selling skills" in it, and say, "We work in the area of sales training," and again with "team building," and so on. After drawing five or six circles, Bob would slide the legal tablet across the desk to the prospective client and ask, "In which area can I help you the most?"

Bob's is another great example of Creativity in action. He didn't get stuck asking the IQs: "When are we going to get a four-color brochure?" or "Why don't we have the beautiful marketing materials of other training companies?" Instead, he asked the QBQ of Creativity: "What can I do to succeed with the tools and resources I already have?" And succeed he did. Using his simple approach, not only did Bob win our firm's Rookie-of-the-Year award, he also sold more training in his first year than anyone ever had!

But for me, the best part of the story came much later. I shared Bob's story during a session at an insurance firm. A young sales agent ran up to me afterward and said something I hadn't heard before: "Well, John, you got me. You got me good!"

"I got you? What do you mean by that?" I asked him.

"For the last six months, I've been bugging my boss for a bigger, faster, stronger laptop computer." Then he proudly held up a legal tablet and said, "But today I learned I can succeed with this!"

What a shift in thinking! What the young sales agent was really saying was this: "You know, I do that, too. I ask for stuff that I think I can't succeed without." That day, though, he left the session with a completely different view of his situation—and himself. That's powerful.

Practicing the Principle of Creativity requires a similar shift for each of us, and the QBQ can help.

THE QBQ MAKES THE DIFFERENCE

Julie, a high school principal, gave each of her staff members a copy of *QBQ!* to read over the summer. She shared this story:

It seems each fall we begin the school year with computers that are not working properly. Normally I receive several complaints from teachers stating they can't teach their class because they don't have the proper equipment. But this year, thanks to the QBQ, my computer teacher, Tim, practiced personal accountability. Instead of complaining about not having enough working monitors to start his class, he went outside the school and solicited a donation of four monitors. As a result, the students were productive right from the very first day!

This story again shows how QBQ drives a creative shift in thinking. Year after year, people had complained about the computers. But the simple QBQ "What can I do to make a difference?" helped Tim take action and find a creative solution that no one else had.

More important, the story also shows that QBQ can impact even those we would least expect to change. Read the rest of what Julie had to report:

Some information about Tim: He has been teaching for more than twenty years, which makes his effort with the monitors all the more surprising. I expect that type of go-get-'em attitude from younger teachers, but not so much from veterans. The QBQ really works!

It sure does.

Our goals become unreachable only when we stop reaching. If we ask QBQs and keep looking, we'll find ways that are not only different but often even *better.*

Be creative. Keep reaching. You'll find a way.

ADVANTAGE
PRINCIPLE
FOUR

·

SERVICE

CHAPTER FIFTEEN

QBQ! Service: Doing for Others What We Don't *Have* to Do

QBQ!

Michael DeVito had a problem. For months, he and some friends had been planning a weekend hiking trip to the Adirondacks. The Wednesday evening before they were to go, Michael was in Chicago on business when he suddenly realized he had forgotten one very important detail: boots. The Adirondacks in March promised to be cold and wet. Michael had meant to order some new hiking boots but hadn't gotten to it, so here he was, two days before the trip, with no boots. And he was out of town.

So from his hotel room he called L. L. Bean's 800 number. "I don't have a catalog with me," he told the customer service representative who answered, "but

I need a pair of boots I meant to order awhile ago. I saw them in the catalog, so I know you have them."

The woman laughed and said, "We have more boots than I can count, sir. Let's see if we can narrow it down a bit!" Her name was Kristi, and Michael sensed he was in good hands.

The call turned into a friendly conversation as Michael told Kristi about the trip. Together they concluded he probably wanted "cold weather" boots, which whittled the options down to a more manageable dozen or so. Michael then described every detail he could remember from the catalog, and between the two of them they pinpointed three possibilities. They were almost there. Then Kristi asked, "When did you want them?"

"To be honest with you," Michael said, somewhat embarrassed, "I need them by Friday. The trip is this weekend."

"Hmm," she said. "I can't get these out till tomorrow. So our normal two-day shipping won't work. And we still don't know for sure which boots you need."

Michael was starting to lose hope.

Then Kristi saved the day. "Here's what I'll do,

Michael," she said. "Tomorrow I'll overnight you a pair of each of the three likely candidates in your size. You'll get them Friday. Try them all on, pick out the pair you want, and then ship the others back. I'll include a return shipment ticket, all filled out so you can just call the number to request a pickup. Meanwhile, give me your credit card number. I won't charge anything to it until you call me Monday to tell me which ones you took on your trip. How does that sound?"

Long pause.

"Michael, are you there? Would that be all right with you?"

After a few moments of stunned silence, Michael finally responded with, "Wow!"

As Michael told me this story, I could see in his eyes that he had experienced something more than just a company that had met his needs or a person who had gone beyond all expectations. He was sharing something he could still *feel*—and would never forget. When I finally asked him how the camping trip went, he laughed and said, "I don't remember. I spent the whole weekend raving to twelve guys about L. L. Bean!"

A company can't *buy* that kind of advertising! And it all came from one person choosing to go beyond what was expected by doing something she did not *have* to do. That's QBQ Service, and it makes all the difference.

We do *not* engage in Service when we ask the IQs:

"Why are people so demanding?"
"When will customers start following the rules?"
"When will my staff be more motivated?"
"Why can't that department do its job right?"
"When will others care like I do?"

We *do* engage in Service when we ask the QBQs:

"What can I do to understand others' needs?"
"How can I serve the customer more?"
"How can I be a better coach?"
"What action can I take to help them succeed?"
"How can I add value by doing what I don't *have* to do"

Engaging in Service is an essential part of the QBQ spirit, and the advantages extend into every area of our lives. Service strengthens relationships and builds trust. It makes us more effective leaders, both at work and at home, and adds real value to the lives of those we serve, as well as our own. But most important may be the feelings of personal satisfaction and pride that come from rendering Service to others.

CHAPTER SIXTEEN

Service and Humility

Servant *Leadership.* Entire books have been written on the subject. Still, some people struggle with the concept because they believe serving is subservient. But in reality, it's not. Others hear the phrase "servant leadership" and think it's an oxymoron, a contradiction in terms, such as:

Double Solitaire
Civil War
Old News
Unbiased Opinion
Student Teacher
Legal Brief
Adult Child
Pretty Ugly

Those are fun examples, but "servant leadership" does *not* belong on the list. From the QBQ perspective, *servant leadership* means recognizing that humility is the cornerstone of leadership. It's all about having an attitude of "I'm here to help *you* reach *your* goals!" as opposed to "I'm in charge and you're here for me."

Not everyone in a leadership role sees serving as part of the job, of course, but the good leaders do.

ENCOURAGING THE HEART

In February 1986, Jim Strutton hired me to sell leadership and sales training. It was my first job in sales. My assignment was to recruit twenty sales managers to attend a five-hundred-dollar, two-day workshop to be held in May, only three months away. I had to learn fast. I was digging up leads, cold-calling by phone for appointments, working hard. By May, though, only nine people had signed up. On the first day of the workshop, I was discouraged. Jim would be facilitating the session while I watched and learned. After we set up the room, we had a few minutes to wait for the participants to arrive.

Jim looked over the room and said, "You know what, John, I see twenty." Slightly confused I said, "Twenty what, Jim?"

"I see twenty people in this class," he answered.

"Jim," I said, trying to straighten him out, "I only sold nine tuitions."

He smiled and said, "I know, but I see twenty because I know *you* can do it!"

We held the class and I learned a great deal. Jim did a marvelous job, and I saw some sales managers' lives changed. One told me he'd been ready to throw in the towel as a manager and go back to the field, but our workshop renewed his hope and confidence. The experience deepened my belief in what I was offering my clients.

Our next session was scheduled for July, only sixty days away. I never worked so hard in my life. It was like a graduate-school class in *rejection*. If you've ever been in sales, you know exactly what I mean. I remember one day when, after making seventy-five phone calls—reaching only a half dozen prospects and being turned down by all of them—I sat alone in my office (at that time, a furnace room in the basement of my house), laid my head on my desk, and muttered, "This is impossible."

But by the time July arrived, I had sold sixteen tickets. Better, but still short of the objective of twenty. Again, Jim came up to me before the session began and said, "John, I see twenty." My first thought: *This guy really needs to buy a calculator.* He went on to say, "I see twenty, because I know *you* can do it." *Okay, Jim, maybe I can. Maybe I can.*

Thirty days later, I conducted a class for twenty-two managers, and for the next two years never had a class with fewer than twenty.

Yes, I needed to believe in myself—and my potential—but I also needed someone in my life to help me develop that belief. I needed someone to transfer his belief *in* me *to* me, which is exactly what Jim did for me. It took humility on his part, but I heard the message "I believe in you!" loud and clear, and it made such a difference.

What messages do you send to the people around you? Too often—instead of sending positive, encouraging messages like "I see twenty!"—we send *discouraging* messages of doubt such as:

"Did you check your numbers?"

"You said *what* to the customer?"

"Why'd you do it that way?"

"You better just let me handle that."

"Why don't you ever get things done on time?"

"When will you start taking my advice?"

Each of these says: "I doubt your capabilities," "I'm not sure you can do it," or "I don't trust you to make the best decision." When we communicate negative messages like these through our words and actions to people around us, we do more harm than good. And this applies to each of us, no matter our title or position.

Encouraging the heart is a rare skill. It's also a powerful form of Service. Both at work and at home, let's demonstrate humility like Jim and serve others by asking the QBQ "What can I do right now to help them succeed?"

CHAPTER SEVENTEEN

Organizations Don't Serve—People Do

— QBQ! —

Stories of outstanding Service like those of Jim Strutton and Kristi at L. L. Bean seem to be the exception, not the rule. See if any of these more typical scenarios seem familiar:

> I was sitting in a restaurant, talking with friends. When the server came over, I asked cheerfully, "So, what's new in the way of salads?" Her reply? "Most people just read the menu." *Ouch!*

> The pharmacy called to say my prescription was ready. When I arrived an hour later, I saw two long lines, so I jumped into one and waited quite some time. When I eventually

reached the counter, the clerk began rifling through a basket, searching for my order. With no results, he said, "Sir, is your name displayed on our electronic board on the wall?"

"Well, I really don't know," I said. "But you folks told me by phone it was ready so I came right over. I've been waiting a while already."

With that he gestured to my left and said, "I'm sorry. You're going to have to check in with us first over in *that* line." I turned and saw the other line was now so long the last person was in another county. *You can't be serious!*

I was on the phone with my insurance agent, discussing a claim. I told him about the accident I'd just had—my first in years—and the steps I took afterward. He said, "Looks like I need to come over to your house so we can go over the rules again." Go over the *rules*?

Bad service—it boggles the mind. No company would ever declare, "Customer service is a bad idea!" In fact, it would be difficult to find even one organization that doesn't consider Service to be a core value. Yet the problem continues. Why? One reason is because we forget this truth:

Organizations don't serve people, *individuals* serve people.

The individual is accountable for providing outstanding service, and it's the organization's responsibility to fully support them in that effort. Remember—in the customers' eyes the institution is only as good as the person they are interacting with *at that moment*. In other words, the individual *is* the organization.

Whether we define a customer as someone buying goods or services, or expand the definition to include coworkers, the people we lead, and even friends and family, none of us can afford for even one of them to hear the message, "Bad, bad customer!"

Instead of the IQ, "Why don't customers start following the rules?" let's ask QBQs such as "How can I best serve this person at this moment?"; "What words can I use to put them at ease?"; and "How can I make the customer feel special?" That's the way to add value.

CHAPTER EIGHTEEN

Service:
It's the Right Thing to Do

=| QBQ! |=

Greg and Carol were realizing their entrepreneurial dream as the proud owners of two coffee shops in Denver. However, one of the stores was not doing as well as they'd hoped. Despite Greg and Carol's excellent brew and pleasing personalities, their store's location was lousy—and business was hurting.

One morning, there was a power outage on the same side of town as their troubled shop—just what they didn't need! Things were bad enough, and now they couldn't even open up for the day—a direct hit to the bottom line. But instead of getting upset and complaining about it, Greg thought about all the people who were trying to get ready for their day. They had no electricity, no hot water, and—worst of all—*no coffee!* As coffee lovers know, one morning without caffeine is more than an inconvenience, it's a disaster.

Greg made a decision: He drove the five miles to their other store—the one that still had power—and brewed five pots of coffee. Then he took them back to the blacked-out store, set up a table outside, and *gave* away coffee to anyone who came by. When those five canisters were drained, he filled them again and again, until people stopped coming.

"He didn't think about himself for one minute," Carol said, as she told me the story, "or about the fact that we were losing money. It never occurred to him to charge for the coffee; he just wanted to make people smile and he did it. Folks would gladly have paid for their coffee, but Greg said, 'No way! You've had a difficult morning already.'"

What a wonderful demonstration of Service! How easy it would have been for a small-business owner in a tough situation to react differently by asking IQs such as "Why did the realtor sell us this crummy location?"; "When will the local economy improve?"; and "Why can't I find good help?" But people like Greg, who serve from the heart, don't think that way.

By the way, you might expect this story to have a fairy-tale ending, but it doesn't. In the world of business, reality can be harsh. Here's the rest of what Carol had to say: "If you're wondering, that store never made it. We had to shut it down a year later, and it almost put us under. But the people in the neighborhood never forgot us, and I will never forget what Greg did."

In the real world, Service may not always increase our income, win that promotion, lift stock prices, or save the store—but it might just save the day.

Service—it's simply the right thing to do.

CHAPTER NINETEEN

A Legacy of Service

=| QBQ! |=

On May 20, 1975, when I was just sixteen, my father showed up unexpectedly at the gas station where I had a part-time job after school. He was in his pickup truck with my older brother, E.J., and neither of them looked very good. Dad's face was beet red, and E.J. was white as a ghost. I'll never forget the contrast. Dad said, "Johnny, I want you to ride home with us." I told him I'd take a rain check since I had my own car.

"No, ride home with us," he insisted.

"But why, Dad?" I asked. I didn't understand, yet I sensed something was terribly wrong. "What's going on?" I asked cautiously.

"Your mother just died."

I couldn't believe it. I wouldn't believe it. In a futile attempt to deny what I knew I had heard, I said weakly, "You mean *Grandma* died. Right, Dad?" My mom's mother was in her eighties.

"No," he said, gently, "Mom passed away about an hour ago."

My mother, at fifty-one years of age, had suffered a cerebral hemorrhage. In a moment, with no warning, our lives were changed forever. All these years later we still miss her, and I would give anything for her to know my wife, Karen, and our children.

A week after my mother passed away was my seventeenth birthday. In our house, Mom had always been the one to create the birthday atmosphere. With all that had happened that week, I didn't know if anyone even remembered it was my birthday. I just about forgot it myself. As I drove off the family farm that morning for my first day back to school, my father was at the end of the driveway digging a big hole for a tree. I stopped and we spoke, but neither of us mentioned my birthday. I drove on. It was a lonely ride.

Around 10 A.M., over the Ithaca High School intercom, I heard, "John Miller, please come to the principal's office." When I got there, I saw on the front desk a long white envelope. On the outside, written in the black Flair pen my father always liked to use, was my name. I knew what it was—a birthday card. I opened it up and it said, "Dear Johnny, Happy 17th. I love you, Son. We'll get through this!" It was signed "Pop" and inside was a twenty-dollar bill he really couldn't afford to give me.

I can hardly imagine what it was like for him to have suddenly lost his best friend of more than twenty-five years. Yet with all he had on his mind and heart, he set aside his farmwork, changed his clothes, drove seven miles to Rexall Drug, bought and wrote in the card, drove three more miles to Ithaca High, and delivered the surprise—all to show he loved me.

He wasn't a perfect man, but that day so long ago he did a perfectly wonderful thing. Of course, the twenty dollars is long gone, but the memory of what he did for me remains forever.

In April 2002, my dad, Pastor Jimmy Miller, passed away at age eighty. His memorial service, held at the church he preached in for many years, was full to the rafters. Standing room only. When it was over, Karen, the kids, and I stayed another three hours while church people, former wrestlers (he was also Cornell University's wrestling coach for twenty-six years), neighbors, and friends told story after story of what Jimmy had done for them:

"He came and got me at 2 A.M. when my car broke down!"

"He gave me fifty dollars for groceries when I had nothing!"

"He helped me bring in my hay before it rained!"

"He played piano at the nursing home every afternoon for our residents!"

I realized then that my dad had left a powerful legacy of Service for which he'll always be remembered and cherished.

Each of us can do the same. Kristi, the L. L. Bean customer service rep; Jim, my sales manager; Greg, the coffee store entrepreneur; and a father named

Jimmy all added value to the lives of others by doing what they did not *have* to do.

Let's follow their lead. By asking the QBQ, "How can I serve?" we can unleash the power of personal accountability and build our own legacy of Service.

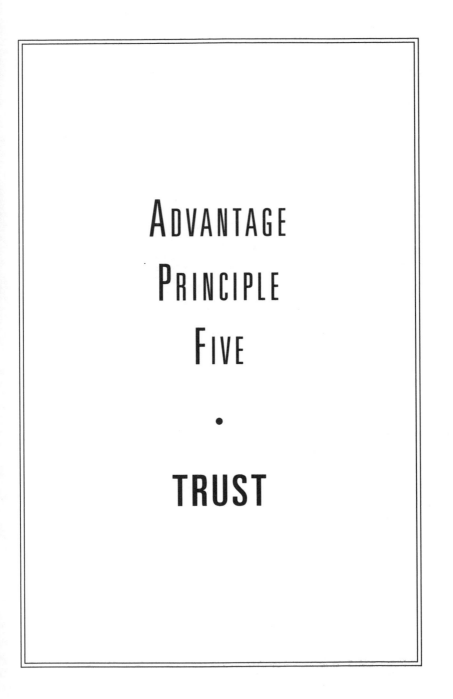

ADVANTAGE

PRINCIPLE

FIVE

•

TRUST

CHAPTER TWENTY

QBQ! Trust: It's Up to Me

=| QBQ! |=

Trust provides a wonderful advantage in our lives. It forms the foundation of strong relationships, which are critical to success both at work and at home. With Trust, we communicate more openly and effectively. We are more creative and collaborative. Our teams are stronger and more productive. Our families are happier. We find more satisfaction in everything we do.

We do *not* build Trust when we ask the IQs:

"Why don't you talk to me more?"
"When will my kids start listening to me?"
"Why won't my staff open up?"
"Who is making all these changes?"
"When are they going to tell us what's going on?"

We *do* build Trust when we ask the QBQs:

"How can I truly understand you?"
"What can I do to know them better?"
"How can I build their confidence in me?"
"What can I do to support the organization?"
"How can I better understand the situation?"

There are many ways to build Trust, but first we must believe that it's our job to do so—that we are personally accountable. Trust grows from our actions as individuals, and each of us is responsible for building Trust in our relationships.

WARNING SIGNS

"How strong is the Trust in your organization?" Whenever I ask this question of a group, most people literally groan. And the groaning tells the answer: "Not very strong." For any leader, that should be a warning sign. Two other signs to watch for are *silence* and *cynicism*.

By silence I mean not raising concerns or objections, not offering suggestions and ideas, not speaking freely. Every individual will have his or her own reasons for not speaking up. But if you find yourself wondering "Why don't people speak up?" you might want to redirect your focus and ask if you have created a culture in which they feel free to do so. I received the following e-mail after a presentation at a firm that had fallen on tough times:

> *In our organization you are quickly accused of not being a "team player" if you suggest anything might be amiss. We've been ordered twice to not question anything the company does because we all have to "work together."*

Few people would speak up in an environment like that, and rightfully so. But the cost to the organization is tremendous: decreased productivity, missed opportunities, low morale, high turnover. The list goes on.

As costly as silence is, cynicism is even worse. Cynicism is not the same as skepticism. When we're skeptical, we doubt something is true or whether an idea will work. It's not personal and can even be healthy at times. Cynicism, on the other hand, is very personal and a huge problem for many organizations. It's when we question someone's intentions, sincerity, and goodwill. Here's the rest of the e-mail:

> *It was just laughable that management would bring you in to talk to us about accountability. If you look at what's left of our "team," the organization has been reduced by 40 percent but almost every VP is still here! How can we trust and respect management after all this?*

The answer is, this person probably can't. Situations like this can make it very difficult for people to trust. The best strategy is to do the work before the warning signs appear in the first place. Ask the QBQ "What can I do today to build Trust?" and get to work. We can't wait for someone else. It's up to us.

CHAPTER TWENTY-ONE

Trust Builders

There are many ways to build Trust. Let's explore some of the best ones now.

TELL THE TRUTH

I wanted to ask a question of Sheryl, a prospective client, but was afraid of seeming pushy. I hesitated, finally saying, "I'd like to ask you something, but I'm not sure how to word it."

Her response was wise: "Why don't you *say* it the way you're *thinking* it?"

Just say it. Speak the truth. What a great idea!

Honesty is a powerful Trust builder. It says, "I respect you. You have the right to know." Also, it's a strong sign of self-confidence to be willing to speak—and hear—the truth.

Most of us were raised to tell the truth, but are we really *honest*? In a training session, the vice president of sales and six regional sales managers were talking about the changes going on in their business. They had some tough news they needed to announce to the field. Suddenly, like a politician caught in a scandal, one said, "What kind of a *spin* can we put on this so the salespeople will buy in?"

So often we speak in code and innuendo. We avoid telling the truth in order to be polite or preserve an illusion. Maybe we fear conflict. Maybe we can't bear to be the "bad guy." We claim that by being less than forthright, we are protecting someone else. But really, we are trying to protect ourselves from the pain of speaking honestly. Some examples:

- A manager tells an employee, "You were passed over for the promotion because you don't have enough years in," instead of candidly discussing critical growth areas.
- A coach tells the team, "You played well, but

the officials made a lot of bad calls," instead of saying the other team was simply better.

- A parent tells her child, "The teacher isn't being fair to you," instead of confronting him about poor study habits.

Whatever the motivation, spinning the message is a Trust killer. Telling the truth, even if it stings, is the best approach. Where there is truth, there is Trust.

SPEAK TO THE RIGHT PERSON

Do you know what "triangling" is? If you haven't heard the term, you've certainly seen the behavior. It's where person A is upset with person B, but rather than speaking directly to B, A talks to person C about B—and then sometimes C tells B what A said! Follow that?

Venting is one thing. Sometimes "blowing off steam" to a third party is the best way to deal with our initial frustrations. Also, some of our feelings may be about our own personal issues and so may never need to be expressed directly to the person at all. But triangling is something else entirely—and it can cause real problems. Even when seemingly innocent, it wastes time and energy, solves few problems, causes hurt feelings, and breeds distrust. Who would you trust more—the person who talks behind your back or the one who comes to you directly?

Got a problem with somebody? Talk to *them*— not someone else. Do it in the QBQ! spirit of respect and humility, of course. Don't discard the notions of diplomacy and being appropriate for the sake of honesty. But talk to them. It may be more difficult, but it's far more effective. And it's a great way to build Trust.

COACH

"As a first-time supervisor I was incredibly aggravated and discouraged," says Valerie, who works for a nonprofit. "I'd frequently ask questions such as 'Why can't we hire reliable and committed employees?'; 'When will my staff open up to me?'; and 'Why don't they seem to care?' But when I went through the QBQ training, I realized how off track I had been.

I wasn't coaching or helping my people, only damaging my relationships with them by blaming and complaining. My approach was hurting the team and preventing each person from reaching his or her potential.

"Now I ask QBQs like 'What can I do to develop my people?'; 'How can I be a more effective coach?'; and 'What can I do to help them win?' And the result is more openness and camaraderie than ever before. I seem to have gained their trust, and the team is more effective everyday. Finally, I feel like I'm doing what I should be doing: Making a difference!"

Coaching is an excellent Trust builder. Listening to someone's goals and dreams and helping them get there by sharing knowledge and experience says, "I want you to succeed. I believe in you."

Whether it's serving as a Little League coach, giving a friend some handy tips, helping kids with homework, or leading the team you manage to new heights, coaching builds trusting relationships that last.

TRANSFER AUTHORITY

It's a crucial moment in the big game. The stakes are high. The ball comes to you and . . . you look toward the team's manager, screaming, "Boss, Boss, what should I do?"

Funny picture, isn't it? But it would never happen, and it shouldn't. Everyone knows the person in the field needs to make the decision in the moment. Unfortunately, we rarely allow people full authority. Here's another scenario:

> You are assigned the task of planning and facilitating an executive meeting. You put a lot of time into it, coordinating with several people, and are looking forward to running the program. Shortly before the big day, your boss decides he doesn't like your plan. He quickly designs his own and tells you he'll now be running the meeting himself.

Can you imagine? I'm afraid you probably can because it happens every day. It's like a yo-yo—the task is delegated to someone, only to be snatched back later. Equally bad is when we hover or watch over someone's shoulder to make sure the project gets done "just right" (translation: our way). Both of these approaches are Trust killers.

Truly empowered people do *not* need to check in with us before they act. Don't say, "Come back to me with three options and we'll decide together." Let *them* decide and act. There are risks, of course, but there are great rewards, too: more ownership, initiative, and creativity, to name a few.

Transferring authority is a great Trust builder. When we give people the authority to decide and act—even to the extent that we let them make mistakes and fail—we have beamed a message straight into their hearts that says, "I know you can do it. You have my complete confidence."

Instead of killing Trust with IQs like "When are you going to do it right?" and "Why do I have to do everything myself?" let's *build* Trust with the QBQ "How can I let go and let them do the job?"

SUPPORT PEOPLE'S DREAMS

Everything in my youth was tied to the sport of wrestling. My dad was a champion wrestler and an Ivy League coach, so I wrestled. He and I both dreamed of continuing the tradition with the next generation of Millers. But when I grew up and married, I ended up with six daughters—and not a natural wrestler in the bunch!

When our only son was born, I was so ecstatic I wanted to name him *Hope*. (Karen, though, felt *Michael* was a better choice. It's safe to say Michael feels the same.)

When Mike was eight, I took him to his first wrestling practice. I quickly realized there was no hope! When we arrived home that evening, Karen asked, "Did you have fun, Mike?"

He immediately wrinkled up his nose and said, "Mom, did you know those other boys are *sweaty*?"

It was over. Finished. He'd never step on a wrestling mat again.

I admit I was disappointed at first, though not too deeply. But even had I been devastated, it would never have become an issue between us, because I have made this commitment to my son: I will never push him to choose any path *but his own.*

When we support others' dreams, it says we respect and care about them. It's a powerful Trust builder, especially when compared to Trust *killers* like, "You actually think you can make a living doing that?"; "Why do you want to go to *that* school? It's not where I went!"; and "When will you start listening to us?" It's not always easy, but by letting Mike be himself and pursue his own dreams, I know a trusting relationship is being built that will stand the test of time.

By the way, what does our only son like to do? The performing arts: guitar, piano, songwriting, drama—and dance. Yes, dance. I have never been so proud of him as I was at a dance competition where he was tapping, pirouetting, and leaping across the stage. He was one of only two males among 173 girls! Mike has genuine talent. If he makes a commitment to the craft, I have no doubt he will excel.

Let's each of us commit to the craft of Trust building. A great way to start is by sending these messages: "I know you can be successful at whatever you choose!" and "I respect and appreciate you just the way you are."

SHOW YOU CARE

One of the most powerful Trust builders of all is demonstrating to others that we have their best interests at heart. Normally, this is not a trait many would associate with salespeople, but then again, Jean was not your average salesperson.

Back in the olden days, before computers and the Internet, Jean sold encyclopedias door to door. One afternoon, she called on a couple about to have their second child. As they welcomed her into their tiny house, she noticed that although it was clean and tidy, slipcovers on the furniture barely hid the wear. The television rested on orange crates, and the curtains were made of old sheets.

During their conversation, the young couple asked questions that indicated real buying interest. Jean, a gifted salesperson, gave them her best presentation. At the end of the visit, the couple signed up for the deluxe package, complete with atlas, annual yearbooks, and a two-tiered bookshelf to house their investment.

Jean was excited! This sale was bound to impress her boss and colleagues since it was going to put her "over the top." She would be number one in the district for the first time. Numero Uno. What a terrific feeling!

In her car she began to complete the paperwork. As she checked over the lines and boxes, she filled in the "Children" box with a one. "Soon to be two," she said out loud. Then she stopped and looked up from the paperwork. Jean thought about that young family and their real needs. The good feeling of making a sale began to evaporate. She stared at their check and thought about being the top salesperson. But she knew what she had to do. As she breathed a deep sigh, she tore the check in half, folded the agreement inside a big envelope, and wrote a message on the back. She put the packet in the couple's mailbox and drove away. The note said, "Thanks for your interest in my products, but I'm wondering with the new baby coming and all if maybe your order can wait. If you still want to go ahead, give me a call. Otherwise, if I'm selling encyclopedias in a couple of years, I'll be back to help you out then."

As it turns out, Jean never did return. While serving as a salesperson, she put herself through medical school and became "Dr. Jean." But I believe if she had gone back, she would have had their complete Trust. She certainly would have had mine.

Showing we care is fundamental to building Trust. Each Trust builder we've discussed in this section sends a message of caring: telling the truth, speaking to the right person, coaching, transferring authority, and supporting people's dreams. They say, "I respect you and care about you." And they each demonstrate that we value others and are sincerely interested in their success.

Putting Trust builders into action will help us build strong, trusting relationships, and each of us is personally accountable for doing so. When we take responsibility for our own actions, when we practice being accountable, when we persistently invest the time in cultivating it—Trust will grow. And our lives will be richer for it.

CHAPTER TWENTY-TWO

Trust Takes Time

=| QBQ! |=

We have seven kids. The oldest four—Kristin, Tara, Michael, and Molly—are our birth children. The youngest—Charlene, Jazzy, and Tasha—are adopted. They are sisters and came to us from the foster care system after they'd been abandoned by drug-addicted parents. They were all under six when they became part of our family.

Soon after our new daughters moved in, Karen was working in the garden while they played nearby. Unknown to Mom, one of them ventured into the "forbidden zone" beyond the lawn. It's the forbidden zone because it's bristling with weeds called goatheads that have incredibly sharp, tough-as-nails thorns that point straight up from the ground. The five-year-old mistakenly went out there and stumbled, landing full force, palms-down right on the goatheads. Indescribable pain! But she didn't react as you might expect and run crying to the nearest parent. Instead, for the next half hour she wandered alone, eyes full of tears, suffering by herself. Eventually, Karen ran across her and couldn't believe what she saw: more than two dozen thorns embedded in her tender hands. It was heartbreaking.

When we shared this story with a child therapist, we asked, "Why didn't she come to one of us the moment it happened?"

The counselor answered with the truth: "She doesn't trust you."

Our first thoughts were *How could that be? We've given her a home, security, food, toys, and—most of all—love!* But the reality was, in her short life, she'd learned she couldn't predict the response of an authority figure. Never being certain how the "big people" in her life might react—possibly with yelling, anger, and shaming words—she had shut down. It was going to take time before she could trust grown-ups—and lots of it.

It's been a few years since the goathead incident, and the girls have come a long way in that time. They're different children now. More open, more joyful—much more trusting. And the growth we've seen in them is not a testament to Karen and me but simply to the fact that building Trust takes time. There are no shortcuts. Even if we're doing all the "right" things, Trust is still not going to appear overnight.

We've learned a lot about Trust from our adoptive daughters. For one, Trust is a delicate state that can be shattered in an instant by a single hurt or disappointment. And rebuilding broken Trust is the hardest job of all.

Furthermore, Trust is a state of mind—a belief that has everything to do with expectations and predictability. When we say, "I trust you," what we're really saying is "Based on your past behavior, I expect you'll act in my best interest, that you won't hurt me or let me down." Or in an organizational setting: "I'm confident you'll do a good job on this project. I can rely on you. I'm comfortable giving you this responsibility."

Trusting relationships bring rewards that perhaps go beyond anything else we've discussed in this book—but they don't come easily or quickly. So be patient. Be persistent. And, above all, be prepared to invest the time it takes to build Trust.

LIVING
THE
ADVANTAGE
PRINCIPLES

CHAPTER TWENTY-THREE

Living Like Larry

—| QBQ! |—

In *Flipping the Switch,* we have said that asking QBQs is like flipping a switch that unleashes the power of personal accountability and brings to life Learning, Ownership, Creativity, Service, and Trust. Throughout the book, we've shared many examples of activating these Advantage Principles and how that gives us a powerful edge in everything we do. Here is one more story that came to us from Thom, a frequent traveler. His tale speaks volumes about the value of flipping the QBQ switch.

It was 10 P.M. in Albuquerque, and my flight home to Tucson through Phoenix had been delayed due to bad weather. My new estimated time of arrival was 2 A.M. But things quickly improved, thanks to an airport security offi-

cer named Larry. He will forever raise the bar for TSA officers at airports everywhere!

Larry was directing passengers to several lines for baggage X-ray and security checks. What was totally surprising, however, was his enthusiastic approach to the job. Instead of mechanically pointing travelers to line number one or two, Larry proudly introduced himself to thirty or so exhausted passengers by shouting, "Good evening, everyone, my name is Larry. I'll be helping you through security tonight. And just so you all know, it's my birthday!"

Well, I couldn't contain myself after seeing and feeling his enthusiasm, so I shouted back, "Happy birthday, Larry!" He giggled and said, "It's not really my birthday, I just love the attention!" Then, like a maître d' in a fine restaurant, he asked the folks next in line, "How many in your party?"

They replied, "Three."

He responded, "Smoking or non?"

Meanwhile, a new line had been opened. As he waved several people into it, he quoted the movie Finding Nemo by chanting, "Just keep swimming, just keep swimming!" Everyone cracked up! By now, I couldn't help but be amazed at how Larry's attitude buoyed so many weary travelers. Then to the group behind me he declared, "Hi, *everyone! I'm Larry!" And like a group attending a self-help seminar, the crowd enthusiastically replied in unison, "Hi, Larry!" As they moved toward the scanners, he joyfully delivered their instructions. I continued on to my gate as Larry's cheerful voice faded into the background.*

And the best part was watching the other TSA officers working nearby. They were smiling from a distance, wanting to have as much fun as Larry—but not knowing how. What a shame that the only thing holding any of us back from being more like Larry is . . . ourselves!

This story is a terrific example of personal accountability in action. Instead of asking IQs like "When will these people learn the rules?"; "Why don't I get paid more?"; and "Who stuck me on this crummy shift?" Larry embodied personal accountability by asking QBQs such as, "What can I do right now to serve my customers?" and "How can I exhibit enthusiasm for my job?" He made a choice to have fun that night, and his choice delighted many people.

Larry demonstrated the power of the Advantage Principles. He took Ownership of his attitude and role by using his Creativity to delight the people around him. He built Trust with his customers by providing great Service that clearly came from the heart. And I would bet money that he's committed to lifelong Learning. People like Larry rarely consider themselves "finished products."

Living the Advantage Principles made Larry stand out from his coworkers in only positive ways. Though we don't know whether this brought him an "Exceeds" rating on his performance review (as with Bill, whom we met in chapter 1) or a promotion, it's easy to imagine the personal advantages that come from displaying such energy and enthusiasm for life. Living like Larry would be a worthy goal for anyone.

Finally, this story is a reminder of the importance of taking action. Throughout this book, we've seen time and again how personal accountability gives us an advantage in virtually every area of our lives. But these changes will not happen without our effort. Just as electricity doesn't magically appear out of nowhere to run our homes and businesses, personal accountability won't magically appear in our lives. It's up to us to do the work. Each of us must dig the trenches, lay the wire, install the equipment, and, finally, flip the switch.

As we come to the end of our time together, one final question remains—one last QBQ to send you on your way:

What specific actions will I take today to unleash the power of personal accountability in my life?

Ask the question. Flip the switch. See for yourself the difference the QBQ! Advantage Principles will make.

Appendix

Putting the Advantage Principles into Action

The following questions and exercises can be used alone or to stimulate group discussion. They are designed to encourage reflection on the content we've explored in this book and to help convert knowledge about the Advantage Principles into action.

PERSONAL ACCOUNTABILITY AND THE QBQ!

Chapter 2
1. What does personal accountability mean to you?
2. What leadership roles are you currently playing in life?
3. What are the three guidelines for creating a QBQ?
4. Identify five IQs you have asked in the past and convert them to QBQs.

THE ADVANTAGE PRINCIPLE OF LEARNING

Chapters 3–5

1. Which of the five Roadblocks to Learning is your biggest stumbling block, and what problems does it cause you?
2. Have you ever not heard someone because of Exclusion? What could you have learned from them?
3. In what way, if any, do you feel entitled? How does this impact your life?
4. What lessons have you been trying to share with others that actually might apply more to yourself?
5. In Robin's story, we discovered Learning equals change. What changes will you now make in yourself? What might the rewards be?

THE ADVANTAGE PRINCIPLE OF OWNERSHIP

Chapters 6–12

1. Identify a problem in your life. What IQs do you ask that prevent you from taking Ownership of the situation? What QBQs could you ask instead to help you practice the principle of Ownership?

2. Read chapter 7, "The Blame Game," again. In what ways do you blame others? How does this affect you?
3. Referring to chapter 8, what is an "us against them" mentality costing you and your organization?
4. In chapter 11, we talk about the importance of a "no excuses" approach to safety. What other areas of your life might benefit from a "no excuses" attitude?
5. Have you ever used the Ultimate Excuse—"It's not my job"? Now that you've read about Ownership, how would you handle the situation differently?
6. Have you ever taken the principle of Ownership to the extreme? What additional problems did it create for you?

THE ADVANTAGE PRINCIPLE OF CREATIVITY

Chapters 13–14

1. What, if any, IQs do you ask that prevent you from practicing Creativity? What QBQs could you ask to make Creativity a more natural and regular part of your life?

2. Think of a situation you are facing today that might benefit from Creativity. What action could you take to be more creative?

3. What tools and resources do you lack that you believe you need in order to reach your goals at work or at home? In what other way could you accomplish those goals?

THE ADVANTAGE PRINCIPLE OF SERVICE

Chapters 15–19

1. What did you learn about Service from Kristi at L.L.Bean? How can you apply this in your life?

2. Think about the worst customer service you ever received. How did it make you feel?

3. Do you believe Greg, the coffee shop owner, did the right thing that morning? What would you have done?

4. Do you know anyone who needs encouragement? What can you do to help?

5. Why is a legacy of Service a worthy goal?

6. What can you do today for another that you do not *have* to do?

THE ADVANTAGE PRINCIPLE OF TRUST

Chapters 20–22

1. What specific idea about Trust challenged your thinking the most? Why was it challenging to you?
2. Does silence or cynicism exist in your home or workplace? What steps could you take to eliminate these telltale signs of distrust?
3. Have you ever hovered over someone while they performed a task? If so, how do you think it affected them?
4. Identify a current example of triangling in your life? What impact is it having?
5. Think of someone you know who really takes the interests of others to heart. What can you learn from this role model about Trust building?

Visit www.QBQ.com today!

At QBQ.com you can:

- Explore the complete QBQ! training system.
- Send a QBQ! Kudos e-card to someone you know.
- Download the QBQ! "Panic Button" to provide QBQ! inspiration when needed most.
- Purchase books.
- Subscribe to QBQ! QuickNotes! (free e-mail stories of personal accountability).
- Recommend QBQ.com to others to spread the word on personal accountability.
- Participate in our accountability polls.
- Inquire about John G. Miller speaking to your group.

QBQ, Inc.
*Helping Organizations Make Personal Accountability
    a Core Value*
Denver, Colorado
303-286-9900 or 800-774-0737
Fax: 303-286-9911
E-mail: staff@QBQ.com
www.QBQ.com

Share QBQ! with Others

Helping businesses, organizations, and families
make personal accountability a core value

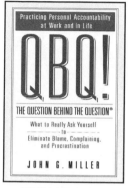

ISBN 0-399-15233-4

ISBN 0-399-15295-4

AVAILABLE JANUARY 2006

Penguin Group (USA) Inc. books are available at special quantity discounts for bulk purchases for sales promotions, premiums, fund-raising, or educational use. Customized books or book excerpts can be created to fit specific needs.

To order bulk copies for give-aways, premiums, distribution to employees, sales promotions, or education, contact:

PENGUIN GROUP PREMIUM SALES
PHONE: **212-366-2612**   FAX: **212-366-2679**
www.penguin.com/corporatesales

For fund-raising or non-bookstore resale, contact:

PENGUIN GROUP SPECIAL MARKETS
PHONE: **212-366-2612**   FAX: **212-366-2679**

To order individual copies, contact:

PENGUIN GROUP CONSUMER SALES
PHONE: **800-788-6262**   FAX: **201-256-0017**

Thanks to you for
being willing to Flip
the QBQ! switch!
It makes all the
difference!

John G. Miller

QBQ!